FLYING THE FRONTIERS OF SPACE

FLYING THE

Illustrated with photographs

FRONTIERS OF SPACE

Don Dwiggins

DODD, MEAD & COMPANY • NEW YORK

PICTURE CREDITS

Bell Helicopter Textron, 106; Douglas Aircraft Co., 26, 37, 39, 46 (bottom), 78 (top); Don Dwiggins, 14, 30, 53, 73, 81, 95, 121; General Dynamics, 51 (bottom), 52; Lockheed Aircraft Corp., 19, 97; Martin Marietta, 89; McDonnell Douglas, 92; NASA, 18, 21, 25, 33, 34, 36, 45 (top), 47, 49, 51 (top), 54, 59, 60, 61, 62, 63, 82, 83, 84, 85, 86, 87, 88, 94, 98, 99, 102, 103 (top right), 103 (bottom left), 104, 105, 108; Rockwell International, 68, 69, 70, 103 (top left), 109, 110, 111, 112, 113, 115, 116, 117, 118; The Smithsonian Institution, 15; USAF, 10, 12, 13, 16, 17, 22, 23, 38, 40, 41, 42, 45 (bottom), 46 (top), 48, 50, 55, 56, 57, 58, 64, 65, 66, 74, 75, 76, 77, 78 (bottom), 79, 80, 90, 91, 93, 100, 103 (bottom right); Chuck Yeager, 29.

2 3 4 5 6 7 8 9 10

Library of Congress Cataloging in Publication Data

Dwiggins, Don.
  Flying the frontiers of space.

  Includes index.
  Summary: A history of American experimental aircraft and space vehicles from 1947 to the present.
  1. High-speed aeronautics—Juvenile literature. 2. Supersonic planes—Juvenile literature. 3. Reusable space vehicles—Juvenile literature [1. Aeronautics—History. 2. Airplanes—Testing. 3. Space vehicles] I. Title.
TL551.5.D9   629.1'09'04   81-17388
ISBN 0-396-08041-3   AACR2

The author wishes to thank his many friends in aerospace who assisted in compiling this record of America's conquest of the sky, from the first supersonic flight of Chuck Yeager on October 14, 1947, to the successful orbital flight of the space shuttle *Columbia* in April, 1981. Public Information people at NASA, the USAF. and aerospace contractor facilities gave full support to this effort, to show how it all began at a lonely Mojave Desert place called Muroc. Special thanks go to Ralph Jackson at NASA/Dryden Flight Research Center; to Ted Bear at Edwards Air Force Base; and to Richard P. Hallion, whose authoritative book *Dryden: The History of a NASA Research Center*, prepared for the Smithsonian/National Air & Space Museum, proved to be an invaluable source of early material.

*This book is dedicated to those heroic aerospace pilots
who gave their lives that mankind would one day find a new home
in space through the nation's Space Transportation System*

Contents

Foreword

Watching space shuttle *Columbia* gliding to its historic landing at Edwards Air Force Base on April 14, 1981, was a personal thrill for me. It had been thirty-four years since I landed the Bell XS-1 there on October 14, 1947, after my first supersonic rocket flight. Between those two flights, much has happened at Edwards and its neighbor facility, NASA's Dryden Flight Research Center, to keep America in the forefront of aerospace research and development.

I am glad to have been a part of that program, and to have known so many wonderful people who dedicated their lives to bringing supersonic, hypersonic, and space flight to the beginnings of a whole new era, opened by *Columbia*. Among those newsmen who covered our early flights, I remember Don Dwiggins as a good friend who did his part in accurately reporting the work we did at Muroc.

In this book Dwiggins covers the full story well, bringing to a new generation of young people a bit of history we all shared, in laying the groundwork for America's new Space Transportation System.

—Chuck Yeager
Brig. Gen. (USAF, Ret.)

Captain Charles E. "Chuck" Yeager, USAF, cracked the sonic barrier over Muroc Dry Lake in 1947 in the Bell XS-1.

one / Eyes on the Sky

October 14, 1947, dawned as a beautiful autumn day on the Mojave Desert of Southern California. Jackrabbits scampered across the parched land. Sidewinder rattlesnakes coiled in the shade of greasewood bushes. Above, the morning sun rose higher, beating down on a vast, table-flat alkali expanse called Muroc Dry Lake. Its 301,000-acre surface was ringed with grotesque Joshua trees where wild birds nested in spiny branches.

Suddenly, at precisely 10:26 A.M., at 20,000 feet above the blazing desert a tiny, bullet-shaped plane dropped away from a silvery B-29 bomber, shot up to 43,000 feet, and rocketed toward the unknown. Down below, the peace and quiet were quickly shattered by a thunderous *BOOM!* that caused desert rodents to dive for their holes.

It was history's first man-made sonic boom. The sound of the future. The opening salvo in man's exciting race for space. The plane that caused it was called *Glamorous Glennis*, a Bell XS-1 rocket ship named for the wife of the pilot, Captain Charles E. "Chuck" Yeager of the United States Air Force.

At that historic moment, Chuck Yeager had become the first pilot to "break the sound barrier." Later, when the USAF delivered *Glamorous Glennis* to the National Air and Space Museum in Washington, D.C., its chief of staff, General Hoyt Vandenberg, would say that "the XS-1 marked the end of the first

Edwards AFB was called Muroc Flight Test Base during World War II.

great period of the Air Age and the beginning of the second. In a few moments, the subsonic period became history and the supersonic period was born."

The XS-1 did far more—it proved the value of the research aircraft as a flying tool, one that uses the sky for a laboratory, one that would open the way for airplanes to free themselves from the bonds of earth's gravity and fly off into outer space.

In fact, the XS-1's tailfire blazed a trail across the sky that would lead through such unknown territories as the so-called "thermal thicket," as future winged aerospace craft called space shuttles flew off into deep space itself.

The United States' race for space goes back to the year 1911, only eight years after the Wright Brothers opened the Air Age with their short flights at Kitty Hawk, North Carolina, in a frail little biplane. By 1911 Americans had discovered that other nations were far ahead of them in aeronautical research, and World War I was on the verge of exploding. In that year proposals were made to establish aeronautical laboratories in this country to catch up, but it took four years to set up the National Advisory Committee for Aeronautics. NACA was given the job of establishing wind tunnel laboratories to study aircraft models, and a flight-test facility to work with full-size problems.

Not until 1917, with World War I raging, was our first national flight laboratory, Langley Research Center, established, near Hampton, Virginia. It served the country well in the early days of aviation, but more room was needed to train military pilots and flight-test new planes. However, it was September, 1946, when NACA decided to send a small band of engineers and technicians from Langley to Muroc, to assist the Bell XS-1 supersonic research program.

Muroc has an interesting history that goes back to the turn of the century, when the lake bed was called

Air Force test pilots set world speed records over Muroc Dry Lake in 1940s, following speed course marked in oil.

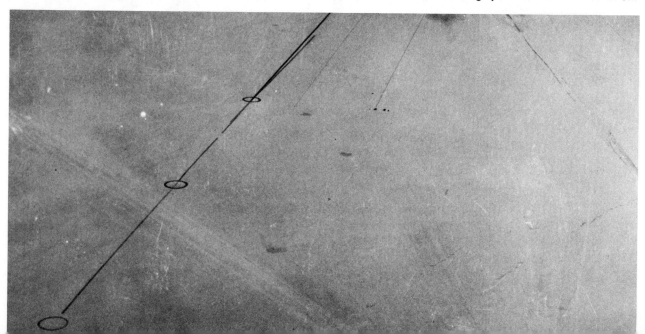

"Pancho" Barnes was a Hollywood stunt pilot in early years.

Rodriguez, after a local gold mining camp. Shaped like an hourglass, the alkali bed in winter months is covered with two or three inches of water. Desert winds wash it back and forth, polishing the bed as smooth as a billiard table.

But ten months of the year the lake bed is bone dry, making it the world's largest landing field for even the heaviest aircraft. In 1910 Rodriguez was renamed Muroc, when a family of farmers named Clifford, Effie, and Ralph Corum settled there. They simply spelled their name backwards and Muroc was born.

In the early 1930s Muroc was used by aircraft designers and pilots to try out new planes, and in 1933 it became a bombing range for Army pilots from March Field down near Riverside. A race pilot named Florence "Pancho" Barnes flight-tested Lockheed planes there, and bought herself an 80-acre ranch nearby, which would become a social center for military pilots who enjoyed horseback riding—the Happy Bottom Riding Club.

One day in 1935 test pilot Wiley Post made a forced landing there in his research plane, *Winnie Mae*, wearing his famous "man from Mars" pressure suit. He scared the daylights out of H. E. Mertz, a Muroc storekeeper out in his sail car, when he staggered up asking for help in unscrewing his clumsy helmet. Another strange apparition came to Muroc in 1940, when designer John K. Northrop dropped in with his N1M, the first Flying Wing. There would be more, many more, funny airplanes darting across the skies of Muroc, but perhaps the strangest sight of all was a 650-foot-long battleship that appeared on the dry lake in 1943—the *Muroc Maru*.

A battleship? Well, sort of—at least a wooden replica of a Japanese Navy heavy cruiser, built as a target for World War II pilots to aim at during bombing and strafing practice runs. From a distance, visitors

Muroc storekeeper H. E. Mertz was on the dry lake in his sail car when test pilot Wiley Post landed his *Winnie Mae* research plane, wearing his "tin can" pressure helmet, and asked for help getting it off. When Mertz saw him he ran away, scared half to death.

Muroc Maru was a 650-foot-long wooden mock-up of a Japanese battleship, built on the dry lake as a bombing target in World War II. In winter months water covered the lake bed and it looked real.

were startled by the undulating mounds of dirt alongside the *Muroc Maru* and shimmering heat waves that created a mirage effect—people swore they'd seen it riding at sea on an inland lake! The *Muroc Maru* was finally dismantled as a flight hazard by Army engineers, who first had to rid its hull of unexploded bombs.

During the war years, the Army would move its major aeronautical research and development center from Wright Field in Ohio to Muroc, for reasons of security—they needed a place to flight-test America's first jet plane, the Bell XP-59A, a twin-jet single-seater that used the British Whittle engine developed by General Electric. Bell test pilot Robert Stanley first flew the XP-59A on October 1, 1942, and the United

States was officially in the Jet Age—at Muroc. (While being readied for its first flight, a wooden propeller was attached to the nose of the XP-59A to disguise the fact that it was a jet plane.)

Facilities were primitive then. The Muroc control tower, known as Oscar Junior, was a single Hallicrafter radio plugged into a 110-volt extension cord and installed in a guard shack set precariously on two sawhorses. Sometimes it blew over when the winds were high. But it was busy. Controllers in Oscar Junior kept track of two newer jets—Lockheed's XP-80 Shooting Star, dubbed *Lulu Belle*, and XP-80A, the *Gray Ghost*.

With the war drawing to a close, the site became known as Muroc Flight Test Base, and on February 12, 1948, as Muroc Air Force Base, when the United States Air Force was created. Its name would be changed to Edwards Air Force Base the next year, in honor of Captain Glen W. Edwards, killed in the crash of a Northrop YB-49 Flying Wing. The name remains Edwards AFB today.

Muroc would become an important research center after the war, when a number of advanced design

America's first jet plane flew at Muroc on October 1, 1942. Bell XP-59A was piloted by test pilot Robert Stanley.

NASA's Dryden Flight Research Center occupies north end of Edwards AFB. Note runway 225 on lake bed.

On January 8, 1944, Lockheed test pilot Milo Burcham climbed into the cockpit of the first jet Shooting Star, the XP-80, and asked project chief Kelly Johnson for instructions. "Find out if she's a lady or a witch," Johnson said. She hit 504 mph and they decided she was a lady—so named her *Lulu Belle*.

First Lockheed P-80 delivered to the Air Force, called the *Gray Ghost*, flew at Muroc in September of 1944, and flew so well the Air Force ordered another 5,000.

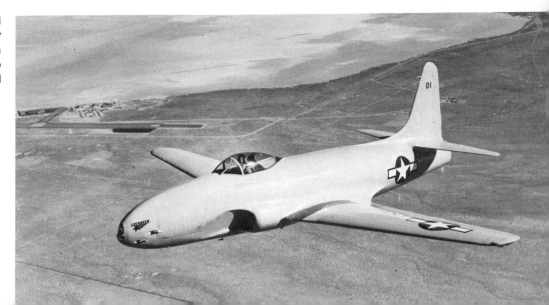

concepts had been developed to push aircraft speed limits closer to what was then known as the "wall of sound"—the speed that sound travels through the air, known as Mach 1, after Dr. Ernst Mach, an Austrian physicist who experimented with supersonics.

The name "sonic barrier" became a part of the folklore of flight when a British scientist remarked that sonic speed "looms like a barrier" against the further development of flight as jets began exceeding 500 mph and approaching an unknown area called the transonic region.

There was good reason to fear the "sonic barrier." In the early postwar years, jets began nosing into a phenomenon called compressibility as they flew at higher and higher Mach numbers, and its effects were disastrous. On September 27, 1946, British test pilot Geoffrey de Havilland, son of the great designer of the same name, attempted to set a world speed record in an arrow-shaped craft, the Swallow DH-108. He flashed across the Thames Estuary as onlookers stared skyward. Suddenly the plane disintegrated before their eyes, and it was ten days before de Havilland's body washed ashore.

Attempts to solve the sonic barrier problem in wind tunnels were fruitless—the tunnels simply choked as high-speed air was forced through them. A slotted tunnel design finally solved the problem somewhat, but a better way had to be found, and the answer was simply to design a supersonic airplane that could use the whole sky for a wind tunnel.

Such an aircraft had been conceived at Langley by NACA engineers as a jet-propelled research plane with razor-thin wings that might knife through the sonic barrier. In 1944 one NACA scientist, Dr. Robert T. Jones, independently worked out an idea for swept wings. His idea was that it might fool the air into thinking it was flowing over a very thin wing section, and delay the dangerous, sudden drag rise that occurs when flying through the transonic region. He figured that the nose shock wave, streaking back like a cone, would pass along the swept wing's leading edge.

There were those who argued for the swept wing and those who favored a razor-thin straight wing for a supersonic design. Others argued whether the power should be supplied by a jet or a rocket engine. It was

Efforts to solve the sonic barrier problem in wind tunnels were fruitless, as the tunnels choked on the high-speed air, until slotted vanes were added. This 16-foot transonic tunnel was built at Langley Research Center.

Northrop Flying Wings first flew at Muroc in 1940. Captain Glen W. Edwards died in the crash of a YB-49 Flying Wing, and Edwards Air Force Base was named in his honor.

decided that not enough was known about swept wings in 1946, and no jet engine was then available for the job of "punching through" the sonic barrier.

The engine chosen for the job was developed by Reaction Motors, Inc., of New Jersey, and consisted of four separate rocket chambers clustered together. Each produced 1,500 pounds of thrust. The Bell aircraft company was given a contract to develop the first supersonic research plane, XS-1, and it would have straight, thin wings. But how would it be launched? The XS-1 had a high-pressure fuel system that burned up rocket fuel so fast there would be no time to take off, climb to altitude, and go supersonic. It would have to be dropped from a "mother" plane.

The Bell XS-1 was a conservative design, shaped like a bullet, its structure able to withstand punishing forces of 18 G's—eighteen times its normal weight. It had retractable gear for landing, if not for takeoff. The fuel, alcohol and liquid oxygen, would be forced from their tanks to the engine under pressure of 2,000 pounds per square inch from a dozen spherical nitrogen bottles. The system was so heavy it displaced much fuel, so only enough was left for 2½ minutes of flight.

Lockheed's XF-90 penetration fighter first flew at Muroc on June 6, 1949. It had a needle nose, jet exhausts running back to the tail, wings flush with fuselage bottom. With two J-34 jet engines it could fly 667 mph at 1,000 feet altitude.

Another feature of the XS-1 was an all-moving horizontal tail surface, to provide solid control at transonic speeds, and when it rolled out of the Bell factory, the question was where to fly it. The winter months of 1945 had left Muroc "dry" lake under several inches of water, so the decision was to fly it at Pinecastle Field, near Orlando, Florida.

Bell test pilot Jack Woolams rode the XS-1 to 27,000 feet in the belly of a Superfortress mother plane, cut loose for a power-off flight, glided down and completely missed the runway. It was obvious that a bigger landing field was needed—Muroc. Although the XS-1 project was a Bell-Army Air Force affair, NACA decided to transfer thirteen engineers and specialists from Langley to the West Coast as the NACA Muroc Flight Test Unit to support the effort. It was the forerunner of today's National Aeronautics and Space Administration's Flight Test Center.

The XS-1 was not alone in its assault on the sonic barrier in 1945. It was joined by the Navy's Douglas D-558 program and another three Army programs that would eventually evolve as the X-2, X-3, and X-4 projects. And in Germany, an abandoned Messerschmitt project was being revived as the future X-5 project.

The XS-1 and the D-558 programs were coming up to the line neck and neck, with two different approaches. Where the XS-1 was designed to punch through the sound barrier with brute force, the D-558 was more conservative, designed for a high cruise at transonic speed. In fact, they would well complement each other on future test flights for this very reason. Where the XS-1 was air-launched, the D-558 would take off like a conventional airplane and fly on jet power, not rocket power. A second design, the D-558-2 Skyrocket, would be rocket-powered and use swept-back wings.

On October 7, 1946, the second Bell XS-1, with its XLR-11 rocket engine installed, left Bell's Niagara Falls plant for Muroc, secured in the bomb bay of its Superfort launch plane, and the first flight at Muroc was scheduled for October 10. The flight was aborted, but the next day Bell test pilot Slick Goodlin completed its maiden glide flight without incident.

It was not until December 6 that Goodlin made the first powered flight in the XS-1, reaching a speed of Mach 0.79 at 35,000 feet and outrunning his chase plane, a Lockheed P-80. The original XS-1 #1 arrived

The Navy/Douglas D-558-1 Skystreak flew at Muroc as a jet research plane in transonic investigation.

at Muroc, and by May 29, 1947, both planes had completed the contractor program after 20 powered flights.

Now it was time for the AAF and NACA to run their own flight-test programs with the two XS-1s, a joint effort in which both military and civilian pilots would participate. It was a good arrangement—NACA needed military support to get the planes built, and the military needed the technical advice and consultation that only NACA could provide.

The big question now was—who would be the first pilot to go supersonic? Bell's company pilots, Jack Woolams and Slick Goodlin, felt one or the other would be chosen, but the Army and NACA had other plans. The choice was left up to Colonel Albert Boyd, a veteran Air Force test pilot who had just set a

The Douglas D-558-2 Skyrocket had both jet and rocket engines, took off from the ground in assault on the sonic barrier.

world speed record of 623.738 mph in a modified Lockheed P-80R jet. His choice was a twenty-four-year-old test pilot from Hamlin, West Virginia—Chuck Yeager.

Captain Yeager was a double fighter ace from World War II. Flying Mustangs in combat against the Luftwaffe, he'd shot down an ME-109 and an HE-111K before being shot down himself in March, 1944, on his eighth mission. Flight Officer Yeager evaded capture in occupied France with the help of the French Underground and was interned in Spain.

Released to the British at Gibraltar and flown back to England, he returned to his old squadron, the 363rd FS, 357th Fighter Group, flew 56 more combat missions and shot down another 11 enemy planes, before returning home to attend Test Pilot School at Wright Field.

And now Yeager faced a new kind of enemy—the unknown perils of cracking the wall of sound in the XS-1.

two / *Breaking the Sound Barrier*

Before Chuck Yeager could take the XS-1 all the way through the sonic barrier on full rocket power, there were some familiarization glide flights to be made. On August 6, 1947, he rode the little red bullet up to drop altitude beneath the B-29 mother ship, piloted by Major Robert L. Cardenas.

Lieutenant Robert "Bob" Hoover, who later became a well-known North American test pilot, rode along in the B-29 as the XS-1 alternate pilot to observe the drop. Hoover was aghast at what happened. He later wrote:

"This guy Yeager is pretty much of a wild one, but I believe he'll be good on the Army ship . . . On first drop he did a couple of rolls right after leaving the B-29! On third flight, he did a two-turn spin!"

There was more admiration than shock in Hoover's reaction. After all, it took a certain quality to be a great test pilot, and Yeager had it. He had the cool confidence and aggressiveness of a fighter pilot, and an instinctive feel for what an airplane was going to do. By August 29 Yeager had fully checked out in the XS-1 with a powered rocket flight to Mach 0.85, and was ready for the big one.

In September the NACA Muroc Flight Test Unit became a permanent facility under NACA's new Director of Research, Hugh Latimer Dryden, an internationally known aerodynamicist. Under Dryden, the unit would grow to become the nation's top civilian flight research base, with the XS-1 program headed up by Walt Williams.

Captain Chuck Yeager named the Bell XS-1 _Glamorous Glennis_ after his wife, became first pilot to fly faster than sound in it on October 14, 1947, at Muroc Dry Lake.

Yeager now bore down on the big job at hand—taking the XS-1 supersonic. After making the acceptance flight on the thicker-winged XS-1 #2 on September 25, Yeager got to work on XS-1 #1 (serial number 6062), a saffron-colored bullet on which he painted the name _Glamorous Glennis_ after his wife.

On Friday, October 10, Yeager took _Glamorous Glennis_ deep into the transonic region, reaching an indicated Mach number of 0.94 on the plane's eighth powered flight, with no sweat. But, gliding back to

Muroc, an opaque coating of frost covered the inside of his canopy, blinding him to the outside world! His chase pilots, Bob Hoover and Dick Frost, got on the radio and talked Yeager down to a safe blind landing on the lake bed. Later, technicians examined the plane's flight recorder and found he'd actually hit Mach 0.997. He'd touched the wall of sound and lived!

It's difficult today to recall that back in 1947 the sonic barrier was a real thing feared by nearly all pilots, with the exception of gutsy research airmen like Chuck Yeager, who felt sure they could break through into supersonic flight. Passenger planes like the Concorde SST now regularly fly at twice the speed of sound and more, but the world of supersonic flight was a fearsome, unknown region back then.

Diving P-38 Lightnings had punched into the transonic region in power dives and experienced weird things like control reversal and inertial coupling—situations where nothing worked like it was supposed to, and attempts by the pilot to correct things only made them worse.

But Yeager didn't buy trouble—he did his job and made decisions on how to handle each unique problem as it came up. Early in October he knew he was ready to go for broke. He had a feeling that things would get better, not worse, when he cracked the sonic barrier. But he couldn't be sure.

On the Friday night after his October 10 flight to Mach 0.997, Chuck and Glennis Yeager drove over to Pancho Barnes' Happy Bottom Riding Club for a steak cookout and a late evening horseback ride. Returning, they raced for the barn, but failed to see in the dark that someone had closed the gate. Chuck's horse crashed into it, throwing him over its head and breaking two ribs.

Yeager thought fast. If the base medics learned he's busted two ribs, he'd be grounded, and the onslaught against the sonic barrier was scheduled for Monday, October 13! Glennis drove him over to nearby Rosamond, where a private physician examined him, taped up his chest, and told him to "take it easy for a month." Yeager thanked him and they drove home.

On Monday the Air Force Muroc Group and NACA were all fired up for the big flight, but a look at

Air Force pilots formed Supersonic Club at "Pancho" Barnes' nearby Happy Bottom Riding Club. Florence Lowe Barnes is flanked on her left by Chuck Yeager, with Frank K. "Pete" Everest on her right. Others (from left, standing) are AF Majors Jack Ridley, Ike Northrop, Clarence Anderson, with Gus Askounis at the keyboard.

the weather decided them against it—too windy. The flight was postponed until the next day. On Tuesday morning, October 14, conditions were perfect. At dawn the sun rose hot and red over the eastern ridges, but not a breath of air stirred across the dry lake bed.

Yeager was already there, checking over the XS-1 with the ground crew. As a gag they'd presented him with glasses, a rope, and a carrot—they'd heard about his horseback accident but did not know he was still in intense pain from two broken ribs. He watched quietly as the crew backed the XS-1 into the loading pit and wheeled the B-29 drop ship over it, winching the XS-1 up into the bomb bay. They carefully fueled it with 293 gallons of diluted ethyl alcohol and 311 gallons of liquid oxygen, or lox. Crew Chief Jack Russell coated the windshield with Drene shampoo to prevent another frost buildup during the glide back to land.

When all was ready, Yeager climbed up into the B-29 where his flight engineer, Captain Jack Ridley, who knew of his predicament, grinned and handed him a length of broomstick handle. "You'll need this, Chuck," he whispered. "You can't close the door with that bad arm!" Cardenas fired up the four Wright R-3350 piston engines and the big bomber moved forward, belching smoke.

Bob Hoover and Dick Frost fired up their P-80 chase planes, but the field was closed to all other traffic. NACA technicians readied their SCR-584 radars and telemetry equipment to track the flight as the B-29 climbed slowly into the morning sun. At 5,000 feet altitude, Ridley helped Yeager climb down into *Glamorous Glennis'* cramped cockpit. He managed to close the door with the broomstick handle. He felt suddenly very much alone . . .

If all went well, Yeager knew his flight would be historic, but he was not one to dwell on dramatics. He was a research pilot pure and simple, carefully probing the unknown. And he was well ahead of his "competition"—the long, sleek Douglas D-558-I Skystreak that had first flown eight months earlier.

Powered with a General Electric TG-180 turbojet, the Skystreak on August 20 was flown to a new

Seven top research planes at NACA Flight Test Center and Edwards AFB in late 1940s included, clockwise from left: Bell X-1A, Douglas D-558-1 Skystreak, Convair XF-92A, Bell X-5, Douglas D-558-2 Skyrocket, Northrop X-4, with Douglas X-3 at center.

Second Bell XS-1 was later modified as the X-1E, with thinner wings, was used for research in aerodynamic heating, stability, and control studies.

world speed record of 640.7 mph by a U.S. Navy pilot, Commander Turner Caldwell, and five days later a Marine jock, Major Marion Carl, hit 650 mph with the second Skystreak.

Both the XS-1 and D-558-I were aiming at the world of supersonic flight, though a sister Douglas research plane, the D-558-II Skyrocket, which had yet to fly, would have both jet and rocket power. And where there was no provision in Yeager's *Glamorous Glennis* for escape in case of trouble, except through the small side door, both the Skystreak and Skyrocket had jettisonable nose sections.

For reasons of its own, the XS-1 project was placed under tight security by the Army Air Force (AAF) and by NACA. Already there was growing competition between the United States and Russia in air and space flight projects, and America was playing its cards close to the vest, as poker players say.

But now, at 10:26 A.M. on the bright morning of October 14, 1947, Chuck Yeager had thoughts only for the grim task ahead—penetrating the sonic barrier he'd briefly touched four days earlier. NACA radar had just cleared the Superfort for the historic launch, and in the B-29 Ridley had raised Chuck on the intercom: "You all set?"

Yeager, wincing against the pain in his ribs, replied: "Hell, yes—let's get it over with!"

Cardenas voiced the countdown from the B-29 cockpit as he dove for speed, in a shallow descent to 20,000 feet pressure altitude, indicating 250 mph.

Suddenly Yeager felt *Glamorous Glennis* drop free. The XS-1 fell away from the dark bomb bay, into the brilliant sunshine, pitching gently down. Yeager's eyes scanned the panel, his fingers went to the rocket engine firing switches, checking each one. The XLR-11's four rocket chambers ignited briefly, then Yeager shut down two to save fuel, raised the nose, and headed for the high sky on the other two rockets.

Pulling away from chase pilot Dick Frost's P-80, Yeager fired the other two chambers and under full 6,000 pounds thrust streaked higher and higher, trailing a cone of fire, with bright yellow shock diamonds visible in the exhaust wake. Farther back, ground observers could see a broad, white contrail, the tiny XS-1 at the apex of the arrow against a pale blue sky.

Glamorous Glennis grew lighter by the second as its rocket engine gulped fuel hungrily, and so flew faster and faster. Yeager watched the needle of the Machmeter flick past 0.8 to 0.9. He gently tried the all-moving stabilizer, checking its reaction as the XS-1 plunged headlong into the transonic region. All seemed well.

At 35,000 feet Yeager shut down two cylinders to conserve fuel and began to ease out of the climb into level flight. Now he fired one of the two shut-down cylinders. The XS-1 streaked smoothly ahead under 4,500 pounds thrust, and at Mach 0.97 the Machmeter needle suddenly hesitated, then jumped ahead to Mach 1.06. The bow shock wave had slipped back across the XS-1's nose and Yeager was through the sonic barrier!

He pressed his mike button and yelled: "Wow! You guys had better get a new Machmeter—I just busted this one!" It was Chuck's way of telling the world secretly that the sonic barrier was simply a myth. For a bit more than 20 seconds the XS-1 plunged smoothly across the sky in supersonic flight. There had been no violent buffeting. He shut down all power and coasted up to 45,000 feet, executed a stall maneuver, then headed for home in a dead-stick glide.

To Yeager it all seemed anticlimactic; he felt a bit disappointed that the breakthrough had not been

Douglas D-558-2 Skyrocket leaves vapor trail as it drops away from B-29 carrier ship to fly twice the speed of sound.

more dramatic. Fourteen minutes after drop, the XS-1's retractable landing gear came down and touched the dry lake bed. The X-plane rolled for 2½ miles before coasting to a stop.

Yeager crawled stiffly out of the cramped cockpit and headed home for a well-earned rest, while others at the Muroc base talked excitedly of his accomplishment. That night there'd be a party at Pancho's. She had promised a free steak dinner to the first blow-and-go pilot to break the sonic barrier.

A new era of flight was opened—the Supersonic Age—and man was one step closer to outer space. But much research and development work, and much flight-testing, remained ahead. Yeager, along with NACA's John Stack and Bell's president Lawrence D. Bell, would be awarded the coveted Robert J. Collier Trophy for first achieving supersonic flight.

Yeager went one step beyond on November 6, 1947, in reaching Mach 1.35, or a bit over 890 mph, at 48,000 feet, and with the AAF program completed, it was NACA's turn to set records with the second

Douglas D-558-2 Skyrocket could take off from ground, so Navy pilots claimed it was a "true airplane," unlike the Bell XS-1 which they said was "only a rocket" you had to drop.

XS-1, #6063. On October 21, 1947, Herbert Hoover became the first NACA pilot to fly an X-plane at Muroc, on a glide flight, but landed hard and broke the nose gear. On December 16 he flew the XS-1 under power and hit Mach 0.71. He finally went supersonic on March 10, hitting Mach 1.065, more than 700 mph, becoming the first civilian to fly faster than sound.

Yeager meanwhile was pushing back the speed frontier farther and farther, while keeping an eye on the Navy/Douglas Skystreak/Skyrocket program. The D-558-2 Skyrocket, with Scott Crossfield at the controls, would finally hit Mach 2 on November 20, 1953, and interservice rivalry was keen.

"The Navy and Douglas guys were putting out the scoop that the XS-1 was not a true airplane," Yeager recalls. "They said it was just a rocket that had to be dropped from a mother ship, while the D-558 could take off from the ground, and go up and break Mach 1.

"One day a bunch of Navy brass gathered at the NACA center at Muroc, to watch a low, near-sonic

NACA test pilot Scott Crossfield was the first to hit Mach 2,
in a Douglas D-558-2 Skyrocket.
It was on November 20, 1953.

Douglas test pilot Gene May flew D-558-1 Skystreak to impress Navy brass, was outclassed by Yeager in diving XF-86.

flyby, by Douglas Test Pilot Gene May in the Skystreak. I climbed into one of the three XF-86s we had, with the J-35 engines, and was sitting up there at 40,000 feet when Gene got ready for his pass. Well, you know how jealous I am about the Air Force, so when I saw him coming I dove down and passed him like he was standing still. Man, those Navy guys were mad!"

Another time, Yeager said: "It was the day before they first flew the D-558-2 Skyrocket, in February of 1948, and Jack Ridley and I dragged the XS-1 to the south end of the lake bed and filled it to about 60 percent of fuel capacity, enough for 100 seconds. Then I made a ground takeoff and took it supersonic at 23,000 feet in an Immelmann, just to show 'em!"

Yeager would fly the X-1s more than forty times in two years, exceeding 1,000 mph at 70,000 feet, and

Chuck Yeager won the Harmon Trophy for flight in Bell X-1A when he hit speed of 1,650 mph.

on July 20, 1951, he made the maiden flight of the Convair XF-92A Dart, a delta-wing flying test-bed.

One of his wildest flights came on December 12, 1953, when Chuck went all out to break the speed record of Mach 2 set by Scott Crossfield in the Douglas Skyrocket. He was in the Bell X-1A, and the flight nearly killed him. He was well aware that wind tunnel studies had showed that the X-1A could expect severe stability problems flying faster than Mach 2.3, but that only urged him to try it.

Launching from a B-29 mother ship, Yeager climbed the X-1A to 70,000 feet, began his pushover, and leveled off. The sky above was blue-black; he was at the fringe of space. He threw on full power from his XLR-11 rocket engine and shot ahead, well past the danger point of Mach 2.3, finally touching 1,650 mph at 74,200 feet.

Suddenly the aircraft destabilized and entered a slow roll to the left. Yeager corrected, but the X-1A snapped right, then left again. Chuck chopped power, to no avail. Still well above Mach 2, the craft

Above: USAF test pilot Chuck Yeager cheated death in a wild flight aboard Bell X-1A when it tumbled end-over-end.

Right: Bell Aircraft's president Larry Bell greets Yeager after flight in Bell X-1A.

NASA test pilot Neil Armstrong, on November 27, 1957, was first to fly an aircraft equipped with hydrogen-peroxide attitude control rocket thrusters—the Bell X-1B.

tumbled completely out of control, slamming Yeager all over the cockpit. (Yeager said: "We had a moment of anxiety there!")

In fact the X-1A plummeted down more than 50,000 feet in 51 seconds, end-over-end, the snow-capped Sierras flashing across his vision as he wondered where he'd crash. Whipped to more than 11 G's, Yeager cracked the canopy with his crash helmet as he fought doggedly for his life. At 34,000 feet the X-1A entered an inverted spin, and finally Yeager got it into a conventional spin at 29,000 feet, from which recovery was relatively simple.

Jettisoning his remaining rocket fuel, Yeager glided dead stick back to the dry lake bed and landed, after one of the craziest flights in aviation history. His only comment, when he emerged, was: "If I'da had an ejection seat, you wouldn't still see me in this thing!" For the flight, Yeager won the Harmon Trophy, for reaching a speed of 1,650 mph.

The flight proved one thing—conventional aerodynamic controls were useless flying at the fringe of space, where the air was too thin to push against. In the future, small jet reaction controls would be added to the conventional controls, and would be necessary for reentry vehicles of the future, returning from outer space.

The need for reaction controls was emphasized further on September 7, 1956, when USAF Captain Iven C. Kincheloe rocketed the Bell X-2 to 126,200 feet altitude, nearly 24 miles. Above 100,000 feet, Kincheloe felt his craft rolling into a left bank as it hurtled across the blue-black sky in a ballistic trajectory. Wisely he did not try to correct the attitude, for fear of tumbling as Yeager had. And finally, on November 27, 1957, NASA test pilot Neil Armstrong would become the first to fly an aircraft equipped with hydrogen peroxide attitude control rocket thrusters—the Bell X-1B.

Things were moving fast now at Muroc. In 1947, under the National Security Act, the old AAF became the United States Air Force, as an equal partner with the Army and Navy, all three under the Department of Defense. In October, 1958, ten years after Yeager's first supersonic flight in the XS-1, NACA became the National Aeronautics and Space Administration. America was moving closer and closer to outer space, with startling new aircraft. And for this progress, men were paying with their lives.

three / To the Edge of Space

Death hovered over Muroc with black, fluttering wings. Skilled test pilots were giving their lives in the name of progress as the race for space gathered momentum:

- On June 5, 1948, Captain Glen W. Edwards, USAF, was killed flying a YB-49 Flying Wing experimental jet bomber, and Edwards Air Force Base was named for him.
- On July 26, 1958, Captain Iven C. Kincheloe, USAF, who had set a world altitude record at 126,200 feet in 1956, died in the crash of a jet plane at Edwards AFB.
- On September 27, 1958, Captain Melburn G. Apt, USAF, was killed in a flight of the X-2 rocket plane to a record speed of 2,094 mph.

Others would die "with their boots on" at this wild western air base on the Mojave Desert, next to nowhere.

While the X-1 and D-558 projects were first to launch man toward the sonic barrier, others quickly followed as AAF projects. Major ones were Project MX-743 (which became the Bell X-2) and Project MX-656 (which became the Douglas X-3). Others emerged as Project MX-810 (the Northrop X-4), Project MX-813 (the Convair XF-92A), and Project MX-1095 (the Bell X-5). All were militarily inspired and were lumped together as the "X-series" of research aircraft, designed to unfold the mysteries of transonic and supersonic flight.

Bell X-2 was effort to modify the X-1 into a swept-wing research aircraft, but it didn't work.

The Bell X-2 was an attempt to modify the XS-1 into a swept-wing craft, but ended up rated as the most disappointing and catastrophic of all the research aircraft programs.

The Douglas X-3, powered with twin J-34 jet engines, proved unable even to reach the speed of sound and, fully loaded with fuel, could not be air-launched at speeds greater than its own stall speed. It made one flight, on October 20, 1952, and was handed over to NACA to play with.

Captain Melburn G. Apt, USAF, died in crash of Bell X-2 on September 27, 1958, after hitting 2,094 mph.

Douglas X-3 had twin J-34 jet engines, and tendency to pitch, roll, and yaw near speed of sound in "inertial coupling."

Below: Douglas X-3 deploying drag chute on landing at Muroc Dry Lake.

Lockheed F-104 Starfighter made many flights at Edwards AFB.

NACA pilot Joe Walker discovered that the X-3 had a dangerous tendency to pitch, roll, and yaw out of control near the speed of sound—a phenomenon called inertial coupling. The cure was simple—make the tail bigger. If nothing else, it led to the successful design of Lockheed's F-104 Starfighter.

The Northrop X-4 was designed as a semitail-less research plane with a swept wing and no horizontal surface, looking somewhat like the German rocketship Me 163 Komet. It used combination ailerons and elevators, called elevons, for pitch and roll control, plus a vertical fin and rudder.

Two X-4s were built and flown, but the AAF lost all interest in them, too, and turned them over to NACA. The first X-4 was considered a "dog" for mechanical reasons, but the second flew well and

Test pilot Joe Walker explored inertial coupling phenomenon in Douglas X-3, which helped make Lockheed's F-104 Starfighter an excellent fighter.

Northrop X-4 was early tail-less research "Flying Wing" type flown by both Air Force and NACA test pilots.

provided much research data. It had a fatal flaw, though. NACA test pilot Scott Crossfield found that at Mach 0.94 it had a tendency to porpoise up and down wildly. In 1954 NACA gave their X-4 back to the USAF, after 82 flights, with thanks, but no thanks.

NACA test pilot Joe Walker took over the Bell X-5, the world's first successful variable swept-wing test-bed, on January 9, 1952, and with Bell test pilot Skip Ziegler found the wing-sweep idea worked fine—it would later be incorporated into the F-111 fighter and B-1 bomber. The second X-5 was checked out by Major F. K. "Pete" Everest, and NACA test pilot Neil Armstrong flew the X-5 on October 25, 1955, but found difficulty in raising the landing gear. The gear legs and doors jammed, but Armstrong got it down safely. It was immediately retired to the Air Force Museum.

Chuck Yeager flies Convair XF-92A research interceptor, which pioneered the trend to delta-wing aircraft.

Bell X-5 was first successful variable swept-wing aircraft. It was flown by NACA's Joe Walker.

Research with Bell X-5 led to design of General Dynamics variable swept-wing fighter, the F-111. It is seen here with wings extended for takeoff.

F-111 flies with wings swept back 72½ degrees for supersonic flight.

Now that research pilots had explored the mysteries of flight at speeds of Mach 1 and Mach 2, it was time to push on to higher and faster speeds and altitudes, nearer the edge of space. They had encountered and pretty well solved the problems of Mach 2 flying—directional stability, inertial coupling, and so forth. Ahead lay new problems—friction heating of the so-called "thermal thicket" at high Mach numbers, where magnesium and other alloys would be required instead of aluminum skins, and reaction controls in flights at high altitudes where dynamic air pressures (Q pressures) are low.

On November 27, 1957, NACA's Neil Armstrong made the first flight of a Bell X-1B with reaction controls, which later would be used on the Project Mercury spacecraft. Now it was time to look to newer research craft, one of which would be the revolutionary reconnaissance plane, Lockheed's stratospheric U-2, that would be used for spy flights over the Iron Curtain as well as for high-altitude meteorological and environmental research. Much research and development work was done on the "Century Series" fighter planes—North American's F-100 Super Sabre, McDonnell's F-101 Voodoo, Convair's F-102 Delta Dagger, Lockheed's F-104 Starfighter, Republic's F-105 Thunderchief, and North American's F-107, a program that was later abandoned.

On October 4, 1957, something happened that shook the scientific world, and had a profound effect on America's efforts to get a manned aircraft into space. Russia had launched Sputnik I into an earth orbit.

Supersonic B-1 bomber has variable-swept wings, first tried out on Bell X-5 research plane. This is one of four B-1s at NASA/Dryden Flight Research Center undergoing further tests in 1981.

NASA raced to catch up with Russia after Sputnik I was launched, sending astronauts into space aboard blunt-nosed capsules to withstand heat of reentry into atmosphere.

and its eerie BEEP! BEEP! BEEP! electronic signal gave people the impression that the Soviets now controlled the heavens.

An immediate reaction was for the USAF and NACA to dig out a 1954 study for a boost-glide vehicle that could take man into space atop a rocket—a plan that would later be called Project Dyna-Soar (for dynamic soaring). A second reaction was the creation of the National Aeronautics and Space Administration the following October to replace NACA.

While Russia's Sputnik was only a small aluminum sphere the size of a beach ball, weighing 184 pounds, it caused a demand in the United States Congress for action! The politicians were simply unaware of what was going on out on the Mojave Desert, where the name of the game was to put a winged, manned aircraft into space, not a basketball.

Thus, on October 7, 1958, eleven years after Chuck Yeager broke the sound barrier, NASA formally

Dyna-Soar rocket ship was designed to ride into space atop Titan ICBM rocket and orbit the earth by "dynamic soaring"—hence its name. It was never built.

Test pilot Scott Crossfield made first powered flight in the X-15 on September 17, 1959. Here it is carried aloft under wing of B-52. The right wing flexes upward to carry the load.

organized Project Mercury to place a manned space capsule in an earth orbit. Instead of wings to fly with, the Mercury capsule would have a blunt nose like those of ICBM nose cones to handle the extreme heat of reentry. Mercury "pilots" would not "fly" their capsule, but ride in it as passengers.

But if the NASA and USAF people at Edwards AFB were disappointed in the sudden shift of emphasis on manned space flight, they were heartened one week later. On October 15, 1958, the first of three new, ugly, black, rocket-powered, manned research aircraft was rolled out of the North American Aviation plant in Los Angeles—the X-15.

X-15s would carry on where the earlier "X-series" supersonic aircraft left off. Combining all the

X-15 RESEARCH SYSTEM

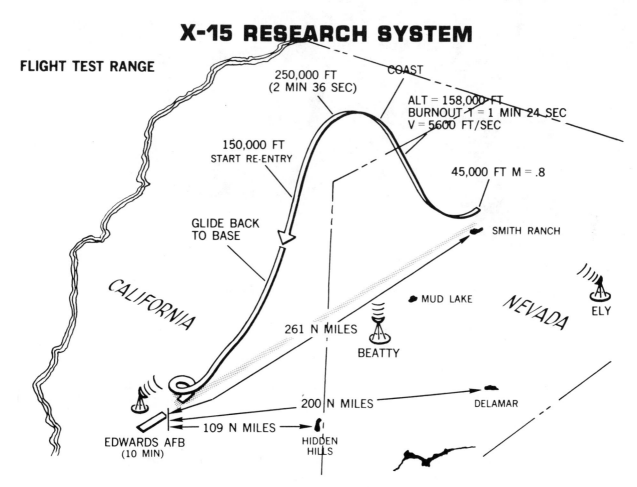

FLIGHT TEST RANGE

250,000 FT
(2 MIN 36 SEC)

COAST

ALT = 158,000 FT
BURNOUT T = 1 MIN 24 SEC
V = 5600 FT/SEC

150,000 FT
START RE-ENTRY

45,000 FT M = .8

GLIDE BACK
TO BASE

SMITH RANCH

CALIFORNIA

MUD LAKE

NEVADA

261 N MILES

ELY

BEATTY

200 N MILES

DELAMAR

109 N MILES

EDWARDS AFB
(10 MIN)

HIDDEN
HILLS

Flight profile of X-15 research system over Edwards AFB flight test range: Drop at 45,000 feet over Smith Ranch, climb to 250,000 feet, reenter atmosphere and glide back to land at Edwards AFB.

X-15 drops away from B-52 with rockets firing for flight into the fringe of space.

technology gained from previous high-speed flight programs, the X-15's designers had produced a breathtaking, rocket-powered aircraft able to probe and explore new frontiers of flight as no other aircraft could, before or since.

Project X-15 dated back to 1954, when two days before Christmas NACA was named technical director of a joint USAF/Navy/NACA team for a cooperative rocket research aircraft program. North American Aviation was selected to build the X-15s.

The big problem in sending aircraft to the fringe of space and beyond was the tremendous energy required to boost them on their way. It was the same requirement that space capsules like Mercury had— to go into orbit. Either manned or unmanned, earth satellites had to reach a speed of 18,000 miles an hour to overcome gravity.

Unlike the Mercury capsule, Dyna-Soar was a winged aircraft with bent-up wing tips and a flat bottom that would be launched on its way atop a rocket, but that still lay in the future. On March 10, 1959, Scott Crossfield, the NACA pilot who had joined North American, made the first captive flight of X-15 #1, to begin "Round Two" of NASA's space plane program, carrying on where the X-planes left off.

While reporters and television crews crowded Cape Canaveral in Florida to cover the exciting launches of Mercury, Gemini, Apollo, and Skylab spacecraft, a still more thrilling space program was unfolding on the Mojave Desert, one that would lead directly to the space shuttles of the 1980s.

X-15 was described as being half-rocket, half-airplane, able to fly to altitudes above 50 miles, which the USAF considered the threshold of outer space. It was an arbitrary figure, for there is no precise altitude

X-15 casts shadow on lake bed as it flares for landing on tail skids, with nose gear extended.

NASA test pilot Neil Armstrong explored fringes of space in the X-15.

where the atmosphere ends and space begins. The air simply gets thinner and thinner, until there is nothing but the deep void of space.

On his first captive flight in the X-15, Crossfield was carried up to 38,000 feet, locked in its launch pylon under the right wing of the B-52 drop ship. Crossfield started up his APUs (Auxiliary Power Units) that furnished the X-15 with electrical and hydraulic power. Suddenly the cockpit filled with smoke! He pressed the mike button and yelled: "Let's go home!"

Smoke in the cockpit was caused by a burned-out generator, but it recurred so frequently that if Crossfield so much as yelled, "Holy smoke!" the mission monitors went ape.

On his first launch on June 5, 1959, Crossfield glided back to Rogers Dry Lake (formerly Muroc Lake)

Wearing NASA markings, X-15 hits Mach 5.38 at 255,000 feet altitude with NASA pilot Bill Dana flying.

and found the X-15 handled well. But on approach to land a dangerous PIO (Pilot Induced Oscillation) set up and the X-15 overshot its touchdown point by a good mile. Mechanics fixed a problem with the booster control system and the X-15 was ready to go for its next flight.

Crossfield's first powered flight in the X-15 took place on September 17, 1959. He tried out his interim rocket engines, two XLR-11s, now boosted to a total thrust of 16,000 pounds. He shot up to 52,341 feet and reached Mach 2.11, or 1,393 mph, when the engines quit, 230 seconds after launch. He glided back safely.

No more troubles developed on Crossfield's second powered flight in the X-15, on October 17, 1959, but on the third flight on November 5, in X-15 #2, there was an engine explosion and fire right after launch. Crossfield landed hard in an emergency touchdown on nearby Rosamond Dry Lake, and the X-15 broke its back.

The first NASA pilot to fly the X-15 was Joe Walker, who flew the #1 ship on March 25, 1960, and hit Mach 2 at 48,630 feet. Again, orbiting spacecraft overshadowed the feat. The week before, Vanguard I

Single-chamber XLR-99 engine replaced smaller XLR-11 four-chamber engine with thrust of Army Redstone missile.

Another view of the XLR-99 engine in the X-15

had completed two years in orbit after traveling 131,318,211 miles and was still transmitting scientific data.

But the pace was quickening over the desert now. On April 13, USAF Major Robert M. White made the first Air Force hop in X-15 #1, and the next month, on May 19, rocketed to 107,000 feet, the highest man had yet flown in the beast. On August 12 he would take the same X-15 to a world altitude record of 136,500 feet, topping the former record set by Captain Iven Kincheloe at 126,200 feet in rocket ship X-2.

Crossfield escaped disaster in X-15 #3 on June 8, 1960, when he ran an engine check on the new, more powerful XLR-99 rocket engine, a huge, single-barrel chamber designed to blast the X-15 to record heights. The XLR-99 had as much thrust as the Army Redstone missile.

USAF and NASA X-15 pilots explored the unknown realm of hypersonic flight. Left to right: Captain William Knight, Lieutenant Colonel Robert Rushworth, Captain Joe Engle, and Milton Thompson, Bill Dana, and Jack McKay of NASA.

In the X-15 cockpit, parked inside a test area surrounded by thick concrete bunkers, Crossfield ran up the engine, shut it down, then pushed the restart button. The engine exploded like a bomb! It slammed Crossfield back against his seat with a force of some 50 G's, scooting the ship ahead 20 feet. Some 900 gallons of ammonia and 60 gallons of hydrogen peroxide fuel—eight tons of liquid power—had ignited simultaneously. Crossfield survived, and was thankful that no one was injured.

The giant rocket engine was next installed in the #2 X-15 and worked perfectly. On November 15, 1960, Crossfield flew it to 81,200 feet, hitting Mach 2.97 or 1,960 mph. A week later he demonstrated the engine's inflight restart capability, and on December 6, after his 14th and last flight in the X-15, turned the ship over to NASA pilots Jack McKay, Bob Rushworth, and Neil Armstrong.

Before 1961 was out, the X-15 had reached its design speed of Mach 6 and flown well above 200,000 feet, but higher, faster flights would be made. The following year saw still newer records made with the X-15—it climbed to 314,750 feet altitude. On November 9, 1962, USAF pilot Robert White had taken it to Mach 6.72—4,093 mph.

During this period of high rides in the X-15, the public's attention was on Cape Canaveral, where John Glenn and other astronauts were riding high in the Mercury capsules. But the X-15 had done far more—it

With rockets blazing, the X-15 was world's fastest airplane.

Major Robert White won his Pilot Astronaut wings by flying X-15 above 50 miles. In 1970 he assumed command of the USAF Flight Test Center at Edwards AFB.

had demonstrated that man could fly an airplane out of the atmosphere into space and back, for precision landings, not just splashing down in an ocean.

It did still more—it demonstrated that a pilot is essential to overcome mechanical problems that may occur in flight. Without a pilot the X-15 would have crashed on 13 of its first 44 flights, according to NASA's Walt Williams. The Mercury and X-15 projects worked harmoniously, however. The former had demonstrated man's ability to function effectively in the weightlessness of space, while the X-15 showed that pilots of future craft like the space shuttle could control a high-performance vehicle in near-space safely.

The X-15 program did something else—it carried 28 experiments out to the edge of space, everything from astronomy to stellar photography and collecting micrometeorites in wing-tip pods. Then in 1964 something new was added. X-15 #2 was rebuilt into a Mach 8 monster, to become the world's fastest aircraft.

There was high drama in this new effort, which followed two X-15 accidents that slowed the program considerably. On November 15, 1967, NASA pilot Mike Adams died when X-15 #3 broke up at high altitude, the wreckage fluttering down amid a rumbling of sonic thunder. The other accident had occurred on November 9, 1962, with X-15 #2, when Jack McKay dropped from the mother ship at 46,500 feet over Mud Lake on NASA's High Range. McKay jettisoned his fuel to make a dead-stick landing on the lake bed after his engine stuck in idle, but everything went wrong—the landing flaps stuck up and he had to land at 290 mph. The gear collapsed, flipping the X-15 over. McKay escaped with his life, but the X-15 needed a total overhaul.

Rebuilt at the factory, the X-15 #2 was lengthened to 52 feet and modified for the addition of two huge external fuel tanks, one holding 6,850 pounds of anhydrous ammonia, the other 8,920 pounds of liquid oxygen. Like later space shuttle launches, the external tanks would boost the X-15 to high altitude—70,000 feet—and Mach 2, permitting it to climb still higher and faster on its internal fuel. Burn time was thus increased from 85 seconds to 145 seconds at 100 percent thrust.

Designated the X-15A-2, the craft was covered with a white heat-protective ablative coating, and on

X-15 #2 was lengthened to 52 feet, and two external fuel tanks were added to increase burn time to 145 seconds at 100 percent power. It became the X-15A-2.

October 3, 1967, high above Nevada, USAF Project Pilot William J. "Pete" Knight launched from the B-52 drop plane brimming with fuel. Dropping like a rock, Knight fired up the big XLR-99 rocket engine, and when the external tanks were exhausted he punched them off, continuing his climb on full power to 102,100 feet altitude.

Level there, Knight shot the X-15A-2 ahead faster and faster, until his Machmeter showed 6.72—4,520 mph, the fastest winged flight ever made! What he didn't know was that the searing heat of 3000 F had incinerated an experimental, strap-on ramjet engine and melted a hole in the craft's ventral fin. Scorching air streamed inside the craft and damaged the propellant jettison system. Nevertheless, Knight skillfully landed safely.

The X-15A-2 would go to the Air Force Museum, but much had been learned during its flights—mainly, that a new kind of thermal protection would be required for future reentry vehicles such as the space shuttle. Two Air Force pilots—Bob White and Bob Rushworth—had earned their Pilot Astronaut wings by flying X-15s higher than 50 miles, where the USAF decided space begins. NASA's Joe Walker also had flown higher than 50 miles, but NASA didn't use the same yardstick to define where space began.

The X-15 project also left its legacy of death. Mike Adams had flown the X-15 #3 to 266,000 feet, well

X-15A-2 drops away from carrier B-52 with Major William J. "Pete" Knight at controls. Aircraft is covered with white ablative material to protect it from extreme heat during record flight to 4,520 mph.

above 50 miles—and pushed over to start his descent when it happened. The X-15 drifted slowly around, end-for-end, then entered a supersonic spin. Out of control, Adams battled for his life, finally stopping the spin, but then the craft began a violent pitching, up and down, so severe that the X-15 was ripped apart, killing the pilot.

The X-15A-2 today holds the all-time world speed and altitude records. Pete Knight's flight on October 3, 1967, to 4,520 mph stood as an unofficial world speed record, and on August 23, 1963, NASA's Joe Walker had flown to 354,200 feet—more than 67 miles above the earth's surface.

The last X-15 flights took place October 24, 1968, when NASA pilot Bill Dana hit Mach 5.38 at 255,000 feet. Then winter rains flooded the lake bed, ending further research flights, and the X-15 program became history.

X-15A-2 is carried to drop altitude under wing of B-52.

four / Flight into Space

Loss of X-15 #3 and the final "dash" speed flights of the X-15A-2 ramjet craft ended the Round Two hypersonic research program at Edwards, and the search was on for a winged aircraft that could fly into outer space for long periods of cruise flight, at speeds of Mach 6 and higher. On Valentine's Day, 1957, NACA formed a "Round Three" study group to find answers.

The X-15s had done well. Among their achievements were the proving of hypersonic wind tunnel theories in actual flight, use of a wedge-shaped tail for directional stability at high speeds, first use of reaction controls for attitude control in space, demonstration of the ability of a pilot to handle a rocket-boosted aerospace vehicle in space and function in a weightless condition, proof that a pilot could safely bring back an aerospace vehicle into the atmosphere.

Something else was needed now—a way to boost an aircraft into outer space on a grand scale, the way giant rockets at Cape Canaveral were boosting blunt-nosed capsules into orbit. The X-15A-2 with its strap-on external tanks had pointed the way.

Since the early 1950s the NACA team had looked into the future to the time when aircraft would fly into deep space itself, and the USAF had already chosen an insignia for its Flight Test Center, showing a dart-shaped craft rushing toward outer space above Mojave with the motto: AD INEXPLORATA—Toward the unknown.

Air Force research planes wear a special insignia with the Latin phrase: AD INEXPLORATA— Toward the unknown.

In the late fifties, NACA and the Air Force had worked on a far-out program, the X-20A Dyna-Soar, after rejecting a plan to build a two-man X-15B as an orbiting spacecraft. Dyna-Soar was inspired by the work of two German scientists during World War II—Eugen Sanger and Irene Bredt. They wanted to build a 100-ton, rocket-propelled bomber launched from a sled. It would fly into space at Mach 10, and return to earth in a semiballistic "skip" trajectory, like skipping a stone across a millpond.

The Sanger-Bredt "antipodal bomber" resembled a slender laundry flatiron, with short, wedge-shaped wings, but the war ended before it could be built. Josef Stalin ordered Sanger and Bredt kidnapped and brought to Russia to develop the spacecraft, but Allied intelligence officers beat him to them, and the scientists remained free in the West.

Wind tunnel tests of a Dyna-Soar vehicle were run at Langley Research Center, and radio-controlled models were dropped from a helicopter to see how they flew. Dyna-Soar used a unique skid landing gear, because ordinary landing gear tires would melt in the heat of reentry, up to 2000° F. An unusual feature of

Dyna-Soar X-20 mock-up built by Boeing is now in Air Force Museum.

Dyna-Soar was its upswept delta wings, forerunners of today's winglets developed by NASA's Dr. Richard T. Whitcomb to reduce wing-tip vortex drag.

A Dyna-Soar study contract was won by Boeing. Its design called for a slender delta wing swept back 73 degrees, two endplate winglets, three elevons for pitch and roll control, a 330 sq/ft. wing area, and a flat bottom. There was room for only a single pilot. Martin won a contract to develop a modified Titan ICBM for a boost vehicle.

At NASA's Flight Research Center at Edwards, test pilot Neil Armstrong practiced Dyna-Soar landing maneuvers in a NASA F5D-1 Skylancer jet, and Milt Thompson was chosen to fly the actual Dyna-Soar. But it was never built. The project was cancelled in favor of another program—the USAF's Manned Orbital Laboratory (MOL). More than $400,000,000 was spent on Dyna-Soar research that would eventually go into building the space shuttles.

Modified NF-104A Starfighters simulated Dyna-Soar landing approach patterns. Craft had small rocket in tail and reaction controls. It was intended to enable pilots to experience weightlessness for two minutes "floating" through an arc at 120,000 feet.

Test pilots at Edwards AFB flew F-104 Starfighter fitted with auxiliary rocket called ZELL (Zero Length Takeoff).

The MOL program, ordered by President Lyndon Johnson, for the first time gave the USAF a specific role in manned space flight operations, and cemented the ties between USAF and NASA when it began in 1963. Earlier, the USAF had come up with a space program called MISS (Man In Space Soonest), which evolved into the Mercury project.

MOL was to have been a 41-foot-long cylinder, ten feet wide, with a shirt-sleeve environment for a two-man crew that would orbit earth for 30 days. Launched by a Titan III-C rocket from Vandenberg AFB on the California coast, it would go into a polar orbit, flying over Russia and China. The USAF astronauts would return in a Gemini-B capsule. But the military nature of the MOL project alarmed the Kennedy administration, and the whole thing was called off.

USAF's Manned Orbital Laboratory (MOL) was designed for launch into a polar orbit, carrying two pilot astronauts. The strap-on booster rockets would drop off.

Orbiting MOL was designed to stay in orbit for 30 days. The two astronauts would then return aboard Gemini capsule.

Below: USAF planned to dock three MOLs together to form space station in earth orbit.

Cutaway view of MOL— Manned Orbital Laboratory

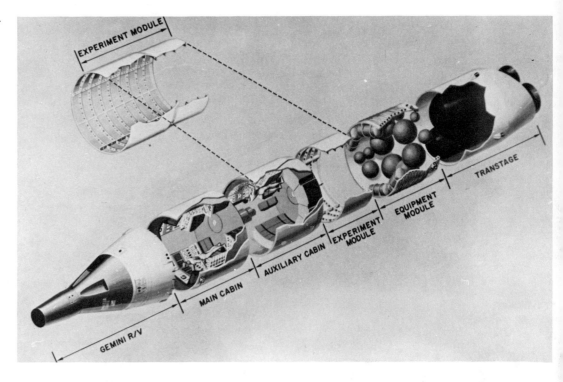

Before MOL was cancelled, Chuck Yeager, now a general, had set up a USAF Aerospace Research Pilots School at Edwards AFB, checking out 41 astronauts, six of whom would undergo an intensive two-year training program to become MOL pilots. Yeager had to scrounge funds to build a space flight simulator from off-the-shelf hardware. Among Yeager's astronaut-trainees were a twenty-nine-year-old Navy Lieutenant Commander, Robert L. Crippen, who would fly the first space shuttle *Columbia* orbit, and Navy Lieutenant Commander Richard H. Truly, also twenty-nine, who was chosen to fly the second space shuttle flight in *Columbia*.

USAF Pilots School at Edwards AFB trained pilots to fly variety of aircraft. Left to right: Row one, Northrop X-4, Convair XF-92A, North American T-28. Row two, Lockheed F-80, Republic F-84F. Row three, North American F-86D, Northrop F-89, Lockheed F-94C. Row four, Boeing B-47, North American B-45, Boeing KC-97. Row five, Convair B-36.

Chuck Yeager, right, and reporter Don Dwiggins inspect the space flight simulator at the Aerospace Research Pilots School. Space shuttle pilot Robert L. Crippen trained in it.

With Dyna-Soar and MOL down the drain, another far-sighted NASA executive dreamed up a new way to go—the unusual Lifting Body program. Paul F. Bickle, who replaced Walt Williams as head of NASA's Flight Research Center in September, 1959, was a former flight-test engineer and sailplane pilot, who set a world altitude record for sailplanes at 46,269 feet in 1961. Like Yeager, he scrounged funds to build a plywood Lifting Body, the M2-F1, and asked an old sailplane buddy, Gus Briegleb, to build it.

The M2 Lifting Body evolved after NASA engineers at Langley tried and rejected a flying saucer craft

NASA pilot Milt Thompson flies plywood M2-F1 Lifting Body in tow behind a DC-3 at 1,000 feet over Rogers Dry Lake.

Gus Briegleb, a veteran soaring pilot, right, built M2-F1 plywood Lifting Body for NASA.

Aluminum M2-F2 Lifting Body flies at 200 mph on approach to land, followed by F-104 chase plane, after drop from B-52 at 45,000 feet.

and the first manned version, the M-1, that resembled a pyramid. The M2-F1 was flat on top and had a rounded bottom. It resembled a rowboat, but amazingly flew well as a glider after being towed aloft behind a car, then a DC-3.

NASA's Milt Thompson flew the M2 on some 100 flights, until in 1964 NASA contracted with Northrop Corporation to build an aluminum version, the M2-F2, followed by the M2-F3, a 22-foot long half-cone without wings that weighed three tons empty. It carried an XLR-11 rocket engine of 8,000 pounds thrust, plus four controllable hydrogen-peroxide rockets to assist in flaring out to land. It was air-launched from a B-52 at 45,000 feet and 450 mph and was designed to fly twice the speed of sound.

The M2-F2 Lifting Body had a strange habit of going into a Dutch roll at low angles of attack, but if you pulled the nose up higher, things smoothed out. On May 10, 1967, NASA pilot Bruce Peterson

M2-F3 Lifting Body is carried to drop altitude by B-52 under its right wing.

dropped away from the B-52 at 44,549 feet and fell like a rock to 7,000 feet, where the craft began its Dutch roll. Peterson pulled up the nose and corrected but, in doing so, overshot his landing. He fired his landing rockets and dropped his gear—too late. The Lifting Body smashed onto the lake bed and rolled over and over at 260 mph. Peterson lost an eye in the accident, but would continue to fly as a Marine Reserve airman.

The damaged M2-F2 was rebuilt as the M2-F3, with a third vertical fin added for better directional control. A jet reaction control system also was added.

NASA pilot Bill Dana made the first flight in the M2-F3 on June 2, 1970, and on December 13, 1972,

M2-F2 was rebuilt after accident as M2-F3, with third vertical fin added to improve directional control.

HL-10 Lifting Body had flat bottom, rounded top, unlike M2s that had flat top, rounded bottom.

made the fastest flight in it—1,064 mph. Altogether the M2-F2/M2-F3 flew 43 times before being retired to the National Air and Space Museum in Washington, D.C.

Another Lifting Body, the HL-10 (for Horizontal Lander), unlike the M2, had a flat bottom and rounded top, with a delta planform. It had three vertical fins, two angled outward, and a tall center fin. The control system consisted of upper body surface and outer fin flaps for transonic and supersonic trim, blunt trailing edge elevons, and a split rudder.

Bruce Peterson had made the first glide flight in the HL-10 on December 22, 1966, and managed to land safely on Rogers Dry Lake after a hairy ride. Later, new leading edges were added for better airflow over the control surfaces. On November 13, 1966, NASA pilot John Manke flew the HL-10 to 525 mph on two of the XLR-11's four rocket chambers, and on May 9, 1969, it made the first supersonic flight of any Lifting Body, flying smoothly. USAF test pilot Major Peter C. Hoag flew it to 1,288 mph, the fastest

HL-10 Lifting Body attached to launch pylon under B-52 wing.

Pilot John Manke lines up HL-10 Lifting Body with runway at NASA Flight Research Center.

HL-10 Lifting Body rockets to 1,000 mph with John Manke at controls of strange wingless aircraft.

Lifting Body flight of all, on February 18, 1970, and nine days later Bill Dana climbed it to a record height of 90,303 feet.

The big question now arose—whether to build the space shuttle with an engine for powered landing approaches like conventional jet aircraft. The test pilots thought otherwise—it would only add extra weight and complexity to the craft.

For starters, NASA engineers decided to try out a powered landing system on the HL-10, replacing the XLR-11 rocket engine with three 500-pound-thrust Bell Aerosystems hydrogen-peroxide rockets, so the pilot could flatten his glide approach angle from 13 to 6 degrees. NASA pilot Pete Hoag made two successful flights, but Hoag found out he was landing faster, had a higher pilot work load, and a degraded mission safety factor. The decision was that the space shuttle would land dead-stick.

NASA's veteran test pilot Milt Thompson explained: "The shuttle, whether it has landing engines or not, must be maneuvered, unpowered, to a point near the destination because the engines cannot be

Lifting Body research program began with seven-foot model called PRIME and designated SV-5D.

started until the vehicle is subsonic and only limited fuel will be available. To us, it seems ridiculous to maneuver to a position where power must be relied upon to reach the runway."

The USAF's Lifting Body research program, X-24A, started up in 1967 with launch of a seven-foot model from Vandenberg AFB down the Pacific test range atop an Atlas launch vehicle. Named SV-5D, it was part of a program called PRIME (Precision Recovery Including Maneuvering Entry). The craft had a flat bottom, rounded top, and vertical fins, was built of aluminum and coated with heat-resistant

Drawing shows the PRIME re-entry test vehicle returning to earth at hypersonic speed.

materials. It too had reaction controls for space flight, and split flaps under its tail for pitch and roll maneuvering in the atmosphere.

The first two PRIME models were lost at sea, but they returned valuable data by radio. The third and fourth models were recovered as they parachuted down near Kwajalein Island in Micronesia.

In an effort further to define the future shape of the space shuttles, Project START (Spacecraft Technology and Advanced Reentry Test) was run in 1965 with six launches down the Eastern test range. The craft were called ASSETs (Aerothermodynamic/elastic Structural Systems Environmental Test) and were employed to test new heat shield materials for space shuttles returning to land. Built by McDonnell

Manned version of PRIME test model became Martin X-24A, a wingless research craft that led to space shuttle design.

Douglas, the delta-shaped ASSETs were constructed of radiative materials such as graphite, zirconium, columbium, and molybdenum, able to withstand temperatures up to 4100° F.

The Air Force next developed a manned version of the SV-5 shape, called SV-5P and given the project name PILOT (PIloted LOwspeed Test). It later became the X-24A, latest in the USAF's X-plane series, and carried an XLR-11 engine. Though designed basically to simulate future space shuttle flight profiles from orbit to land, the X-24A's prime mission was to explore the lower speed regime, from Mach 2 to landing speeds.

On October 14, 1970, the 23rd anniversary of Chuck Yeager's first supersonic flight, NASA pilot John

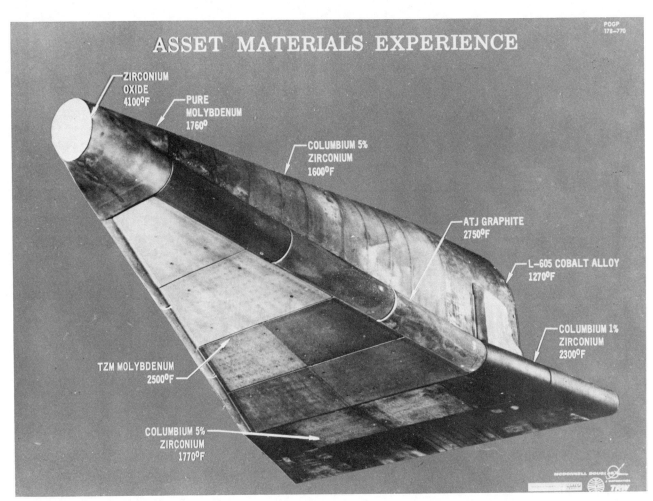

ASSET MATERIALS EXPERIENCE

ZIRCONIUM
OXIDE
4100°F

PURE
MOLYBDENUM
1760°

COLUMBIUM 5%
ZIRCONIUM
1600°F

ATJ GRAPHITE
2750°F

L—605 COBALT ALLOY
1270°F

COLUMBIUM 1%
ZIRCONIUM
2300°F

TZM MOLYBDENUM
2500°F

COLUMBIUM 5%
ZIRCONIUM
1770°F

Research vehicle called ASSET was fired atop rocket to test heat shield materials at temperatures up to 4100° F.

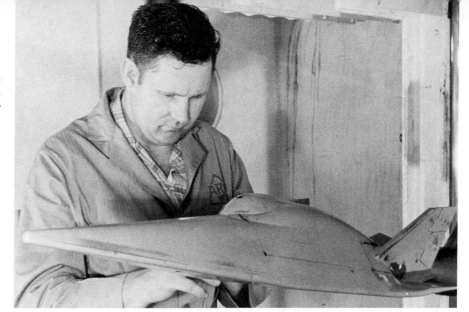

FDL-8X model was tested in supersonic wind tunnel as predecessor of the X-24B for space shuttle research.

Manke rocketed the X-24A to Mach 1.1, reaching 66,000 feet before gliding back down the space-return corridor to an unpowered landing, as future space shuttles would do.

America's last rocket research aircraft, which brought to a close the manned Lifting Body program, was the X-24B, built by Martin for the Air Force and based on a family of reentry shapes evolved at the USAF's Flight Dynamics Laboratory—the FDL-5, 6, 7, and 8. These bodies had a lift-to-drag ratio of 2.5 at hypersonic speeds, meaning they could glide forward 2½ miles for each mile they dropped.

The X-24B was 14½ feet longer than the X-24A and had a 78-degree double delta-shaped wing for better center of gravity control, a boat tail for better subsonic stability, a flat bottom, and a sloping 3-degree nose ramp for hypersonic trim. John Manke first flew the X-24B on August 1, 1973, launching from a B-52 at 40,000 feet. He coasted down at 460 mph and landed at Rogers Lake at 200 mph, precisely where the space shuttle *Columbia* would land one day in 1981.

Mike Love hit 1,164 mph on the X-24B's 16th flight on October 24, 1975, and happily reported that it flew better than any of the earlier Lifting Bodies, handling much like a Lockheed F-104 Starfighter. The

X-24B had slender delta wing, leading to space shuttle design.

space shuttle was now well into its design phase, and mission planners wanted to know whether Lifting Bodies (and space shuttles) would be able to land with precision on a fixed runway, like the three-mile-long one at Edwards.

On August 5, 1975, after making more than 100 simulated approaches in military jets, Manke launched the X-24B at 60,000 feet, and seven minutes later touched down exactly where he had planned on the Edwards landing strip. Using the conventional runway markers, he found it easier than landing on the lake bed.

On September 9, 1975, NASA pilot Bill Dana made the last flight of the X-24B and brought to an end America's rocket research program at Edwards that had begun with Chuck Yeager cracking the sonic barrier back on October 14, 1947. Dana's four chase planes—two T-38s and two F-104s—closed up into a tight diamond formation and streaked down in a noisy salute over Rogers Dry Lake where the long road to the Space Shuttle Era had opened vast new horizons.

Test pilot John Manke used portable cooler to make flight suit comfortable prior to flight in X-24A wingless rocketship.

five / The First "A" in NASA

As the NASA Lifting Body program wound down, Chuck Yeager, commandant of the Aerospace Research Pilots School at Edwards, checked out in the M2-F1 to see how it handled. But when the first actual space shuttles would begin their blistering, searing Mach 25 reentry into the earth's atmosphere from outer space, their pilots would be on their own. No Lifting Bodies or other research craft could simulate exactly the shuttle flights down the reentry corridor. NASA's Flight Research Center had proposed a "mini-shuttle" flight program to validate wind tunnel predictions of the highly critical maneuver, particularly from Mach 5 down through transonic to touchdown at Edwards. But it was decided the effort would cost too much.

Work pushed ahead, however, to accommodate the upcoming space shuttle program at Edwards, with installation of a special "mate-demate" facility for a "piggyback" shuttle/747 carrier-plane combination, and a special electronic microwave landing system.

While work on the space shuttle moved along at the North American Rockwell plant, at Edwards and at other NASA facilities—Langley, Ames, Lewis, and Dryden Flight Research Centers—the government was calling for renewed emphasis on research and development of atmospheric aircraft, under NASA's newly designated Office of Aeronautics and Space Technology (OAST).

"Don't forget," NASA was reminded, "that the first A in NASA stands for Aeronautics!"

NASA's Lockheed-built ER-2 surveys earth's resources.

Already America was well into the commercial jet age, although England, France, and Russia were in the lead in supersonic transports (SSTs) with their Concorde and Tu-144 passenger ships. Both Lockheed and Boeing, encouraged by the highly successful Mach 2 Convair B-58 Hustler bomber program, had built mock-ups of US/SSTs, before they were shot down by environmentalists who demanded that Congress "Ban the Sonic Boom!"

Lockheed also had joined the Central Intelligence Agency to develop a new, faster, Mach 3 reconnaissance aircraft, which emerged as the A-11/YF-12/SR-71 Blackbird program. As recently as 1981, a brand-new, high-altitude aircraft, designated the NASA ER-2 (for Earth Resources), was flying as a spin-off of their U-2 plane, first used to spot forest fires with infrared photographs in the High Sierras.

Other advanced programs had fallen to political pressures—the excellent XB-70 bomber was dead, and the B-1 bomber in suspension, though four B-1s remained at NASA/FRC for research flight projects.

Much could be written pro and con about the experimental North American XB-70A Valkyrie strategic

North American XB-70A Valkyrie was world's largest experimental aircraft, 189 feet long, weighed 500,000 pounds gross. On October 14, 1965, eighteen years to the day after Chuck

bomber, the Lockheed A-11 Blackbird, and other advanced projects involving atmospheric aircraft, but the story here is about the space shuttle and how it evolved, so only a brief look. The XB-70A, incidentally, at the time of its maiden flight was the world's largest experimental aircraft, with a length of 189 feet, 105-foot wingspan, and half a million pounds gross weight.

The XB-70's thin delta wing bent downwards for greater lateral stability at supersonic speeds. Its forward fuselage was built of titanium to withstand supersonic heating, the rest of the craft fabricated from brazed stainless steel honeycomb. Its tires were specially designed not to explode from heat at Mach 3 speeds. On one test flight, part of the wing's skin peeled off at Mach 2.56, and on another a landing gear hydraulic failure forced test pilots Van Shepard and Joe Cotton to make an emergency landing on Rogers Dry Lake.

Yeager's first X-1 supersonic flight, the XB-70A reached design speed of Mach 3 at 70,000 feet. Here it is taking off, flying overhead, opening drogue chutes, skidding to stop.

On a flight of the second XB-70A on June 8, 1966, NASA test pilot Joe Walker flew formation with it in a NASA F-104N Starfighter, while a photoplane flew nearby to take publicity pictures. Walker's F-104N flew in too close, was caught in the B-70A's vicious wing-tip vortex and slammed into the bomber. Walker died in the ensuing crash. The bomber pilots attempted to bail out. Al White, the pilot, made it, but his copilot, Carl Cross, died in the wreckage.

The Lockheed SR-71/YF-12 fared better. On May 1, 1965, five YF-12 pilots racked up seven new world speed and altitude records, and nine world records overall, including maximum speed over a straight course (2,070.101 mph), and maximum altitude for horizontal flight (80,257.86 feet). On June 24, 1971, one joint NASA/USAF research YF-12A experienced an engine fire in flight. Both pilots ejected safely.

While NASA was anxiously awaiting delivery of the first space shuttle, the *Enterprise*, work continued

Air Force pilots tested the YF-12 "Black Beast" at Edwards AFB. It flew at Mach 3 (about 2,000 mph) in sustained cruise flight at 75,000 feet.

on a wide variety of other research projects, each a story in itself. They were, briefly:

- RPVs—Remotely Piloted Vehicles, used in support of General Aviation and other branches of flying, where a high degree of risk to pilot or aircraft favored launch of large scale models up to 30 feet in length. A ground controller flies the RPV just like an airplane modeller with an R/C unit. In June, 1980, one RPV called DAST (Drone for Aerodynamic and Structural Testing) crashed on the Mojave during a wing flutter test. Another, called Compass Cope, was designed as an unmanned, jet-powered, high-altitude, long-endurance craft. Still another was the Firebee II drone, used to run spin tests in ⅜ scale models of craft such as F-15 fighter planes.

- HiMAT—For Highly Maneuverable Aircraft Technology. A powered RPV using an afterburning General Electric J85-21 turbojet engine, with a length of 22 feet and a swept-wing canard configuration. HiMAT featured advanced construction materials such as a composite structure of glass fibers and graphite composites, and metal. A major program, HiMAT is designed to fly at transonic speeds to develop a technology for advanced fighters of the late 1980s.

- Mini-Sniffer—A propeller-driven RPV designed to fly above 100,000 feet to sample exhaust wakes from supersonic aircraft. One was planned to be sent to Mars in a rocket, to sample that planet's atmosphere and take low-level TV pictures of Martian canyons.

- Digital Fly-By-Wire—An advanced flight control system first used in the Apollo space program, designed for future air and spacecraft. Using an F8-C for a test-bed, the system utilizes airborne computers and electronic links from the pilot's control stick to the computers and flight controls.

- Supercritical Wing—A new wing airfoil design that delays the onset of shock waves over the wing that cause a high rise in aerodynamic drag.

- AD-1—An oblique-wing aircraft in which a pivoted straight wing can be turned to various angles to achieve best performance at different flight speeds.

- TACT—A joint NASA-USAF effort called Transonic AirCraft Technology designed to study use of Supercritical Wings on highly maneuverable advanced aircraft.

- PARASEV—A "space-age kite" developed by NASA's Francis M. Rogallo to assist in returning space capsules to earth. Young flyers have adopted it for use as hang gliders and ultralight aircraft.

Remotely Piloted Vehicle model of F-15 Eagle fighter is carried to drop altitude under wing of B-52.

Two NASA research planes fly formation—Digital Fly-By-Wire, followed by Supercritical Wing craft.

Above left: Highly Maneuverable Aircraft Technology (HiMAT) research aircraft is designed as forerunner of fighters for air-to-air combat. **Right:** Propeller-driven RPV called Mini-Sniffer was designed to fly above 100,000 feet to sample air, could be rocketed to Mars to map its terrain with TV cameras.

Below left: Supercritical Wing design is flattened on top to increase wing's lift efficiency. **Right:** Boeing RPV, called Compass Cope, was an unmanned jet plane to be radio-controlled from ground on high-altitude flights.

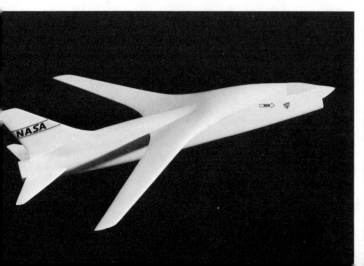

TACT research craft is used to study Supercritical Wings on highly maneuverable advanced aircraft.

Below left: AD-1 Oblique Wing, a NASA test aircraft. *Right:* PARASEV was designed for returning space capsules, was adopted by hang glider pilots instead.

Lunar Landing Research Vehicle (LLRV) was called NASA's "Flying Bedstead," was used to train astronauts for moon landings.

• LLRV—Called NASA's "Flying Bedsteads," the Lunar Landing Research Vehicles used direct jet lift and rocket thrust alone to train astronauts for moon landings. Two were modified as Lunar Landing Training Vehicles (LLTVs). Neil Armstrong, the first man on the moon, was flying one a year before his historic space flight, when it tumbled out of control. He ejected and landed safely by parachute, while the LLTV crashed and exploded.

• Solar-powered Gossamer Penguin—A variation of Dr. Paul MacCready's man-powered aircraft

Solar-powered Gossamer Penguin had 2,800 solar cells to convert sunlight to electricity to run electric motor to turn propeller.

Bell XV-15 tilt-rotor research craft uses propellers like helicopter blades for vertical take-off, tilts them forward to fly as fixed-wing aircraft.

that Bryan Allen flew across the English Channel, it is fitted with 2,800 solar cells that convert light from the sun to electricity to run a motor to turn a propeller to fly the craft. NASA felt it had use in lightweight research aircraft flying at high altitudes.

The list of exciting new projects being studied at NASA/Dryden Flight Research Center seems endless, but these give an idea of the wide range of interest in novel means of flight in the atmosphere and in outer space. Now back to the space shuttle.

six / *The Space Shuttles*

Spaceship *Enterprise* looked nothing at all like the science-fiction television intergalactic patrol craft, but it was in fact an incredible machine. Although also called NASA's Space Shuttle Orbiter Vehicle 101, it would never fly into orbit. Its mission was to fly the Approach and Landing Tests (ALT) at Edwards, carrying on where the Lifting Body program left off.

The goal was in sight now. On March 26, 1976, NASA's Flight Research Center at Edwards was dedicated in honor of NASA Deputy Director Hugh Latimer Dryden, while at nearby Palmdale, OV-101 was nearing completion in Rockwell International's Space Division at the USAF Plant 42.

The public got a first look at space shuttle *Enterprise* on September 17, 1976, when roll-out ceremonies were held at Palmdale. People gasped—it was big as a Douglas DC-9 as it sat in the sun in front of the final assembly building. Its body length was more than 122 feet, it stood 56 feet tall, and had a wingspan of some 78 feet.

Because it would be used solely for approach and landing flights in the atmosphere, after being carried aloft piggyback on a modified Boeing 747, it had no reaction controls, only standard aircraft aerodynamic controls. In January, 1977, space shuttle *Enterprise* made its first trip—overland. Highways were sealed off as the monster craft was trucked 36 miles to NASA/Dryden Flight Research Center.

Reporters and television crews now swarmed over the desert base. Here was big news, bigger than

Space shuttle *Enterprise*, known as OV-101 (for Orbital Vehicle), is mated to 747 carrier aircraft in mate-demate tower at NASA/Dryden Flight Research Center.

Space shuttle astronauts have their hands full monitoring all the cockpit gauges. Note three TV-type CRTs (cathode ray tubes) at center for data display.

anything going on at Cape Canaveral! On February 8, 1977, OV-101 rolled into the mate-demate tower and was hoisted on top of the NASA 747 shuttle carrier aircraft. A week later, taxi tests were completed to make sure the OV-101 wouldn't fall off. Together, the two craft weighed more than half a million pounds.

Readied for its first flight, the OV-101's aft section was covered with a tail cone to reduce drag, and onboard ballast provided a slightly forward center of gravity (CG), with a gross weight totaling 144,000 pounds. Then on February 18, 1977, the first unmanned captive flight was made, with Fitzhugh Fulton at the controls of the 747 carrier ship. For some two hours the mated craft flew over the desert, to a maximum speed of 287 mph and altitude of 16,000 feet. The crew beamed. They could hardly tell the orbiter was aboard!

Sequence shows OV-101 *Enterprise* (left) carried to drop altitude atop 747; (below) lifting off as 747 noses down . . .

After a series of five unmanned captive flights, the first orbiter crew, Astronauts Fred Haise and Gordon Fullerton, took their places in the *Enterprise* cockpit for the first manned captive flight on June 18. All went well.

Spacecraft Commander Joe Engle and Pilot Dick Truly took over for the second manned captive flight. Truly had been one of Yeager's trainees at the Aerospace Research Pilots School, and would later be assigned to fly the second space flight in Orbiter *Columbia* in the fall of 1981, with Engle. On this flight,

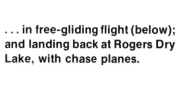

... in free-gliding flight (below); and landing back at Rogers Dry Lake, with chase planes.

the crew tested the Microwave Scan Beam Landing System to check out what is called the AUTOLAND approach. Again the flight was a success. A third manned captive flight was made July 26, with Haise and Fullerton back in the cockpit.

On August 12, Haise and Fullerton made the first free flight in *Enterprise*, lasting 5 minutes 21 seconds, after a climb to 28,014 feet altitude. The aircraft separation sequence was begun at 24,100 feet and 310 mph. Explosive separation bolts were fired as the 747 crew throttled back and opened the wing spoilers to

111

Above, *Enterprise* is carried to
drop altitude atop 747; at right,
diving after separation . . .

. . . above, flaring for landing; and, right, ready for touchdown, with tail cone removed.

slow down. Three seconds later the orbiter crew rolled their craft to the right 20 degrees, while the 747 rolled off to the left.

Going into a dive, the *Enterprise* picked up speed and made two left turns to line up with Runway 17 on the dry lake bed. The landing was smooth, and Haise described the flight as "super slick!"

Engle and Truly made the second free flight in *Enterprise* on September 23, lasting 5 minutes 28 seconds, and tried out the craft's onboard computerized program called TAEM (Terminal Area Energy Management), which constantly evaluated the *Enterprise*'s position, attitude, and velocity (energy) for an automatic landing approach.

After two more free flights with the tail cone in place, Engle and Truly made a flight with the tail cone off, and reported that "the handling characteristics were similar to the tail-cone-on flight, except for the deceleration and speed decrease, due to the increased drag." Astronaut Deke Slayton, NASA's program manager, called it "the most important flight in the whole program." The date was October 12.

Haise and Fullerton made the final tail-cone-off flight in *Enterprise* on October 26, and proved on landing that the orbiter could easily be stopped within the length of Edwards AFB's 15,000-foot runway.

From November 15 through 18, a series of four ferry flight tests were run, and all that remained was for *Enterprise* to be flown back to the Marshall Space Flight Center at Huntsville, Alabama, for ground vibration tests, and to Cape Canaveral for strap-on rocket fitting. Later it was returned to Palmdale, its usefulness ended, to be cannibalized for spare parts for future space shuttles.

Technical and electronic problems would delay the first actual space shuttle orbital flight until the spring of 1981, when on April 12, all systems at Cape Canaveral's Launch Complex 39, Pad A, were GO. Since 1972, nearly $10 billion had been spent on the exciting project, and now the chips were down.

Space shuttle orbiter *Columbia* was first in a planned fleet of spacecraft that would serve in the nation's Space Transportation System as STS-1. There would be no payload, but plenty of instrumentation for measuring the orbiter's performance on its 54½-hour journey in space.

Columbia had arrived at the Kennedy Space Center on March 24, 1979, on a ferry trip from NASA/Dryden FRC in California aboard its 747 carrier plane. In July, 1979, the giant external fuel tank,

Space shuttle *Columbia* being moved to Vehicle Assembly Building for mating with external fuel tanks . . .

154.2 feet high, arrived by barge from New Orleans, Louisiana. It held 143,060 gallons of liquid oxygen and 526,126 gallons of liquid hydrogen. Total weight was 1,667,667 pounds.

Two strap-on solid rocket boosters were attached to the main tank, each containing more than 1,000,000 pounds of fuel. The solid rocket boosters would operate for 2 minutes, along with the main engines, to help the orbiter escape the earth's gravitational pull. At 24 miles altitude, they would separate, descend by parachute, and be recovered from the Atlantic Ocean for reuse. The main tank would be

. . . artist's drawing of liftoff . . .

. . . return to Rogers Dry Lake at end of 54½-hour orbital flight . . .

jettisoned to splash down in the Indian Ocean 8½ minutes into the flight, and would be the only major part of the space shuttle system not reused.

On November 24, 1980, the *Columbia* was mated to its external tank and solid rocket boosters in the huge Vehicle Assembly Building, and on December 29 was moved 3½ miles on its mobile launcher platform to Pad A to await launch, following the countdown conducted in Firing Room 1 of the Complex 39 Launch Control Center.

After more delays, *Columbia* was finally all set for its historic journey into space, and at 7 A.M. on April

. . . and touchdown. In landing *Columbia* functioned as a glider, with no engine to correct its course.

19, 1981, its rockets belching plumes of orange fire and a long white vapor trail, it rose slowly from the launch pad—America's first reusable spaceship.

Strapped in their reclining seats in their pressurized crew compartment, Astronauts John W. Young and Robert L. Crippen were opening a new era in space flight for their country, since the last astronauts flew six years earlier.

For Young, it was old stuff. At fifty, he served as both Chief of the Astronaut Office of NASA and

Commander of STS-1, the *Columbia*. Commander Young already had logged 533 hours and 33 minutes in four previous space flights. In 1972, as Spacecraft Commander of Apollo 16, he had spent more than 70 hours on the moon's surface, driving the Lunar Rover "dune buggy" for 27 kilometers and gathering 200 pounds of moon rocks.

Captain Crippen, like Young a former Navy pilot, had attended the USAF Aerospace Research Pilots School at Edwards AFB under Yeager. On his graduation he remained there as an instructor, until chosen in October, 1966, to join the USAF's Manned Orbiting Laboratory (MOL) program. He had flown jets more than 4,000 hours.

Rising into a northeast orbit, *Columbia* performed well, except for losing a few of the 20,000 silica fiber tiles that had been bonded to the aluminum hull with a special layer of felt, to withstand the expected 2700° F heat of reentry. Veteran astronaut Young's heartbeat stayed steady at from 85 to 90, but Crippen, on his first space flight at forty-three, registered a heartbeat of 130 beats a minute. "A fantastic ride!" he exclaimed.

Twelve minutes after liftoff *Columbia*'s two smaller orbiting maneuvering rockets fired briefly to nudge the astronauts into a low earth orbit, and then fired briefly three more times over the next seven hours to put *Columbia* in its final orbit ranging from 169.8 to 171.8 miles above the earth's surface.

On each 90-minute revolution of the earth, Young and Crippen crossed the equator at angles of 40.2 degrees, so that *Columbia* swept 40.2 degrees of latitude north and south of the equator. Nearing the end of their first orbit, the astronauts opened and shut the two clamshell doors to the 60-foot long cargo bay, where future shuttles will carry artificial satellites and other unique payloads.

Among the payloads to be carried into space by future space shuttles will be experiments chosen as winners in a nationwide Space Shuttle Student Involvement Project, conducted by NASA and the National Science Teachers Association. Objective of the competition is to stimulate the study of science and technology among students in grades 9 to 12. Ten winners from more than 1,500 contestants were selected in the 1980–81 competition.

During the 54½-hour flight through space, Young and Crippen removed their bulky, pressurized emergency escape suits and lived in more comfortable two-piece flight coveralls. They slept in their flight deck seats, rather than in sleep restraints on the lower deck planned for future flights. A carry-on food warmer was used, prior to installing the regular orbiter galley.

After 2 days, 5 hours, 27 minutes of flight, the *Columbia* was turned aft end forward with rocket thrusters, and the craft's main rockets were fired to slow its orbital speed, in its 36th orbit, 169 miles above the Indian Ocean. Over Guam, the orbiter once again was turned around, for the reentry maneuver. Over Wake Island the *Columbia* pitched up to an angle of 40 degrees, exposing the black thermal underbelly tiles to maximum heating.

Now the shuttle was entering the atmosphere, at an altitude of some 400,000 feet, when a 16-minute communications blackout began, due to buildup of electrified gases around the heated craft, which glowed with a cherry color at more than 2700° F.

Crossing the California coast near Big Sur at 138,700 feet altitude, it followed southward along the coastal mountains, crossing the San Joaquin Valley south of Bakersfield at 107,100 feet. Over Mojave it was still flying supersonically at Mach 1.95 and 71,850 feet altitude, raking the desert with a thundering sonic boom.

Next it crossed Rogers Dry Lake at 54,000 feet, still supersonic, but slowing down as it bent around in a looping, 270-degree turn to approach the landing strip from the southwest. Thousands of people covered the desert area watching the thrilling sight, yelling, "Here she comes!" Gear extended, *Columbia* greased onto the runway like there was nothing to it, and rolled to a stop, for a joyous welcome-home celebration.

Touchdown was at 10:21 A.M. local time, and Commander Young's comment was: "It was really a tremendous mission, from start to finish! We're really not too far, the human race isn't, from going to the stars!"

If the comment was rhetoric, it was also somewhat prophetic, for great plans lay ahead for the space

After first orbital flight, space shuttle *Columbia* enters mate-demate tower at Dryden Flight Research Center for checkout prior to ferry trip back to Cape Canaveral.

shuttle, first of the fleet of tomorrow's Space Transportation System. Where the Apollo missions had been purely exploratory, in taking man to the moon and back, the STS Program, which originated 30 years before with the first X-1 flights, had a job to do in space.

The beauty of the space shuttle is that it can be flown over and over and over again, perhaps as many as a hundred times, cutting the cost of space transportation to where it will now become economically possible to exploit space for the benefit of mankind.

Shuttles can carry satellites into orbit and retrieve ones that have quit working. They will ferry giant telescopes above the earth's atmospheric blanket for a better look at the universe. Special cameras will map the earth's resources, and space workers will be carried up to build huge solar energy stations and giant communications stations.

There will be room for as many as four astronauts on the flight deck, with passenger seating and living quarters on a mid-deck. A hatch with an airlock will provide access to the payload bay, or cargo compartment. Provisions also exist for a docking module and transfer tunnel with an adapter, to allow crew members to visit orbiting spacelabs or perform extravehicular operations.

The first shuttle payload was carried into orbit on the second flight of *Columbia* in late 1981, and later military payloads have been planned.

A second space shuttle orbiter, named *Challenger*, was being readied in 1981, to be followed by two more STS orbiters, *Discovery* and *Atlantis*. A great future in manned space flight lies ahead for young men and women, who face a splendid challenge to join the effort to make ours a better world to live in—and above.

Glossary of Aerospace Terms

ABLATIVE MATERIAL—A coating material designed to provide thermal protection to an aerospace craft against friction heat of reentry into the atmosphere.

ABORT—To cut short or break off a flight because of equipment or other failure.

AERODYNAMIC CONTROLS—Surfaces on wing and tail of aerospace craft used to control its attitude by pushing against the air.

ATTITUDE—The position or orientation of a vehicle in motion or at rest.

AUTOLAND—A device to control an aerospace craft during an automatic landing.

BALLISTIC TRAJECTORY—The path followed by a body being acted upon only by gravity and air resistance.

COMPRESSIBILITY—Variation in density of air flowing over a body due to change in velocity.

CONTROL REVERSAL—Effect of compressibility in transonic flight on aerodynamic controls, disturbing their natural function.

CONTRAIL—A visible trail formed in the atmosphere when hot exhaust gases condense into liquid form.

DEAD-STICK LANDING—A slang expression for a power-off landing.

DUTCH ROLL—A flight condition where an aerospace vehicle's wings rock from side to side.

DYNAMIC PRESSURE—Air pressure due to its movement, or movement of a body through it, as that recorded by an airspeed indicator.

DYNAMIC SOARING—Flight without power in which an aerospace vehicle (such as the Dyna-Soar) gains lift flying into denser air at a lower altitude, and "skipping" back up into thinner air.

ELEVON—A horizontal aerodynamic control surface combining the functions of elevator and aileron, as in a Flying Wing.

EXTRAVEHICULAR ACTIVITY—Missions performed by an astronaut outside his aerospace craft.

G FORCE—Symbol representing acceleration due to gravity.

HYPERSONIC—A speed five or more times the speed of sound.

INERTIAL COUPLING—Also called roll coupling. The effect of an aerospace craft movement around one axis being translated to a movement around another axis, as when an abrupt roll produces a "coupled" pitch or yaw. This sometimes happens in craft like the X-3, with a short wingspan and long fuselage, heavily loaded fore and aft, and lightly loaded across the wing.

MACH NUMBER—Ratio of a body's speed with respect to the surrounding air to the speed of sound in the same air.

REACTION CONTROLS—Small jet thrusters on wing tips and nose of an aerospace craft that operate to adjust its attitude when there is no atmosphere for aerodynamic controls to push against.

REENTRY CORRIDOR—The flight path a returning aerospace craft follows reentering the earth's atmosphere from outer space in order to make a precision landing.

ROCKET ENGINE—A reaction engine whose escaping exhaust gases push forward against the engine itself, and containing both a fuel and oxidizer so it can run in absence of air, as in deep space.

SHIRT-SLEEVE ENVIRONMENT—An aerospacecraft's cabin atmosphere similar to that at the earth's surface, not requiring a pressure suit to be worn.

SONIC BOOM—An explosive sound produced when a shock wave formed at the nose of an aerospace vehicle flying at Mach 1 (the speed of sound) reaches the ground. Sometimes two booms are heard, one from the nose shock wave and the other from a trailing shock wave.

SPEED OF SOUND—Sound travels at different speeds through air of different temperatures and densities. At standard sea level pressure it travels 1,087 feet per second, roughly 741 miles an hour. This is called Mach 1, after the Austrian physicist Ernst Mach.

SUPERSONIC—Velocities between Mach 1 and Mach 5 are called supersonic, and beyond Mach 5 hypersonic.

THRUST—The pushing or pulling force developed by an aircraft propeller, jet, or rocket exhaust.

Index